Welcome to a World of Imagination!

Thank you for selecting our book for your coloring journey. As you prepare to embark on this vibrant adventure, we're excited to see the world through your palette.

Artistry Unleashed

Before you dive in, here's a helpful hint to ensure your artwork remains flawless: slip a cardstock behind the page you're coloring. This simple step is your best defense against bleed-through, keeping your creations neat and vibrant.

We Value Your Voice

Finished coloring? We'd be thrilled if you could take a moment to leave your feedback on Amazon. Your review is more than just words; it's a guiding light for fellow coloring aficionados and an invaluable support for us. Let your experience inspire others!

Your creativity gives life to every page. **Thank you for adding your splash of color to our world.**

Coloring book

THIS BOOK BELONGS TO

....

Color testing page

Copyrighted Material